Just a Little D

By Rozlah Ridenoure

Copyright © 2013 by Rozlah Ridenoure

Just a Little Donkey
by Rozlah Ridenoure

Printed in the United States of America

ISBN 9781626970564

All rights reserved solely by the author. The author guarantees all contents are original and do not infringe upon the legal rights of any other person or work. No part of this book may be reproduced in any form without the permission of the author. The views expressed in this book are not necessarily those of the publisher.

Unless otherwise indicated, Bible quotations are taken from the King James Version.

www.xulonpress.com

Dedicated to the Lord. Whom made us just the way He wanted us.

Just a little donkey with big ol' ears,
A tail that is short and stubby,
A shadow of the Cross is on my back.
Some people think I'm kind of ugly.

Virgin Mary is on my back
And Joseph is there to guide me.

Just a little donkey with big ol' ears,
A tail that is short and stubby,
A shadow of the Cross is on my back
Some people think I'm kind of ugly.

Just a little donkey with small black feet
And steps that are sure and steady.

It doesn't really matter what the weather is like
God knows I'm always ready.

Just a little donkey with big ol' ears,
A tail that is short and stubby,
A shadow of the Cross is on my back
Some people think I'm kind of ugly.

Just a little donkey with big brown eyes
And a knack for sensing danger,

Looking for a bed for a new born babe
I took them to the manger.

Just a little donkey with big ol' ears,
A tail that is short and stubby,
A shadow of the Cross is on my back,
Some people think I'm kind of ugly.

Just a little donkey without much pride,
I'm really kind of lowly;

But the Heavenly Father up above
Let me carry something Holy.

Just a little donkey with big ol' ears,
A tail that is short and stubby,
A shadow of the Cross is on my back.
Some people think I'm kind of ugly.

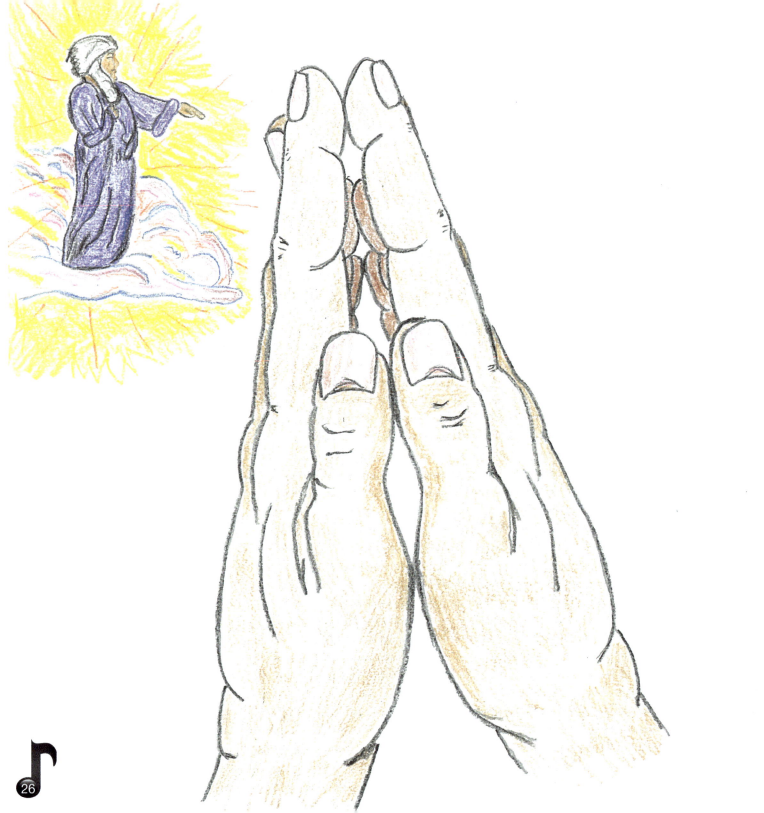

Just a little donkey with big ol' ears,
A tail that is short and stubby,
It doesn't really matter what some people think
Cause my Heavenly Father loves me.

Just A Little Donkey

Chorus:
Just a little donkey with big ol' ears,
A tail that is short and stubby,
A shadow of the Cross is on my back.
Some people think I'm kind of ugly.

I'm on my way to Bethlehem
With a precious load,
Sent down from God Almighty.
Virgin Mary is on my back
And Joseph is there to guide me.

Chorus

Just a little donkey with small black feet
And steps that are sure and steady.
It doesn't really matter what the weather is like
God knows I'm always ready.

Chorus

Just a little donkey with big brown eyes
And a knack for sensing danger,
Looking for a bed for a new born babe
I took them to the manger.

Chorus

Just a little donkey without much pride,
I'm really kind of lowly;
But the Heavenly Father up above
Let me carry something Holy.

Chorus

Just a little donkey with big ol' ears,
A tail that is short and stubby,
It doesn't really matter what some people think
Cause my Heavenly Father loves me.

I will praise thee; for I am fearfully and wonderfully made: marvellous are thy works; and that my soul knoweth right well.
Psalms 139: 14 KJV

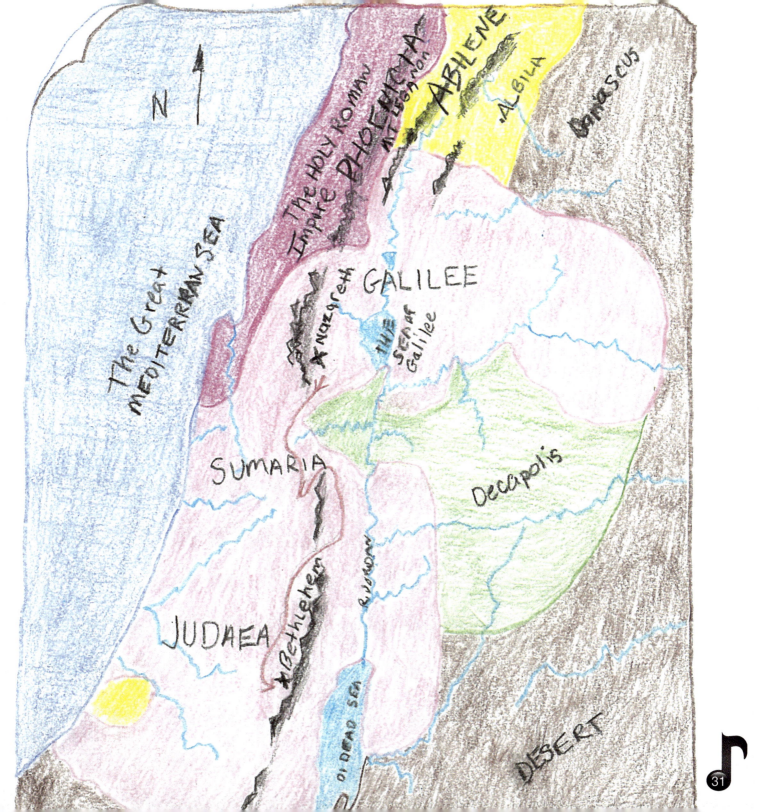

Lightning Source UK Ltd.
Milton Keynes UK
UKOW07f1138010317
295497UK00021B/49/P